THE 4 JOY CHALLENGE

The Gateway To Experiencing a Life of Peace and Freedom

By

Amaka U Ogbonna

THE 40 DAYS

JOY

CHALLENGE

The Gateway To Experiencing a Life of Peace
and Freedom

© 2019 by Amaka U Ogbonna

ISBN: 9781674685861

All rights reserved. No part of this book may be reproduced or transmitted in any form or by any mean, electronic or mechanical – including photocopying, recording, or by any information storage and retrieval system – without permission in writing from the publisher, except for brief quotations embodied in critical articles or reviews.

All Scripture quotations, unless otherwise indicated, are taken from the Holy Bible, New International Version®, NIV®. Copyright ©1973, 1978, 1984, 2011 by Biblica, Inc.™ Used by permission of Zondervan. All rights reserved worldwide. www.zondervan.com. The "NIV" and "New International Version" are trademarks registered in the United States Patent and Trademark Office by Biblica, Inc.™ Scripture quotations marked (NLT) are taken from the Holy Bible, New Living Translation, copyright ©1996, 2004, 2015 by Tyndale House Foundation. Used by permission of Tyndale House Publishers, a Division of Tyndale House Ministries, Carol Stream, Illinois 60188. The Holy Bible, New King James Version, Copyright © 1982 Thomas Nelson. All rights reserved. *The Holy Bible, King James Version*. Cambridge Edition: 1769; *King James Bible Online*, 2019. www.kingjamesbibleonline.org.

I hope you enjoy reading this book. I hope that my mission to encourage a joy-filled lifestyle through this 40 Day Joy Challenge is fruitful. I pray that you live in such a way that you capture joy daily and you consciously seek it.

ii

Acknowledgements

To my parents for introducing me to Jesus, who is now my Lord and saviour. To my Husband, for being an instrument to opening my eyes to a greater version of me. To my children, Diamond and Samuel. To my siblings for their kind support over the years. To my church family. To the family of Christ all over the world.

iv

Table of content

PREFACE.. IX

INTRODUCTION XII

FOREWARD.. XIV

DAY 1..1

DAY 2..4

DAY 3..7

DAY 4...11

DAY 5...14

DAY 6...17

DAY 7...21

DAY 8...25

DAY 9...29

DAY 10...33

DAY 11...37

DAY 12...40

DAY 13...45

DAY 14...48

DAY 15...52

DAY 16...56

DAY 17 59

DAY 18 62

DAY 19 65

DAY 20 68

DAY 21 73

DAY 22 76

DAY 23 80

DAY 24 84

DAY 25 88

DAY 26 92

DAY 27 95

DAY 28 100

DAY 29 104

DAY 30 108

DAY 31 112

DAY 32 116

DAY 33 120

DAY 34 123

DAY 35 128

DAY 36 132

DAY 37 136

DAY 39 ....**144**

DAY 40 ....**147**

PERSONAL THANK YOU NOTE **151**

AMAKATOBY TV RESOURCES **153**

viii

PREFACE

Productive and positive change is as a result of consistent and deliberate repetition of a particular behaviour. Our behaviours are governed by our thoughts. This is why what's going on in our hearts and mind is crucial to truly living a life worthy of all the goodness, potentials and virtue that God has placed on the inside of us. One thing I have found that have hindered many of us from the reality of truly living out the abundant life that God created us to live is the state of our mind. What is the state of your mind? Have you paused recently to ponder on whether there are things in there taking your mind space and not helping you move into the next level and version of yourself that God is calling you to? Most times, it's the negative experience(s) that we've had that have become our barriers. They create negative emotions within us, leading to negative thoughts and resulting to negative actions and behaviours.

This 40 days Joy Challenge is a tool to challenge the reader to a new reality that is totally attainable. YES! Attainable because whilst writing this book, it was as if I was being tested at the same time; Some of which I share later on. The second reason why I believe a joy filled life is attainable is because we all have the power of choice. You can choose joy, stick with it and run with it regardless of what could be going on around you. Your Joy cannot be stolen if you refuse. It's yours! Nothing can actually take it away from you.

THE 40 DAYS JOY CHALLENGE

Think about that. One of the best parts of JOY is that it's free. Now who doesn't like a freebie? It's one of those things money can't buy and most importantly, we have the power to live a joyful life through the help of the Holy Spirit. Acts 1:8 (NIV) says, *"But you will receive power when the Holy Spirit comes on you; and you will be my witnesses in Jerusalem, and in all Judea and Samaria, and to the ends of the earth".*

Sadly, knowingly or unknowingly, we hand our joy out to disappointments that come our way. Yes, face the realities of what you're facing BUT it is so much better to face it with JOY. I pray that this book becomes a tool that you can always go back to during those overwhelming moments that directs you back to the path of living in Joy.

Some Benefits of Living in joy:

- Combats anxiety and depression
- Provides strength and endurance for difficult times
- Gives strength to live by faith and according to your principles and values
- Provides fast recovery from a hurtful situation
- Supports longevity of life
- Able to spread Joy and laughter to the people around you
- Restoration

It may feel foreign and awkward to begin with however not impossible. It always feels awkward when you first begin a thing but if you keep at it, that same thing eventually becomes comfortable and at some point, very easy and normal. So, get as comfortable as you can, fasten your seatbelt and let's take this journey together.

INTRODUCTION

In a world where we've become all too busy chasing goals, ambitions, careers, targets and accomplishments, many have lost the serenity of joy. Our society is infected with the notion that 'success' i.e money is all we need in life and certainly what brings joy into our lives. We are bombarded with the notion that once we can strive and do whatever it takes to become 'successful 'and make a lot of money or buy the biggest house, travel the world, then we can live happily ever after. However, the lie in that is that what is really being sold to us is happiness, if that and not joy. Secondly, we are being short-changed in that we are trading the long term for the short term. Happiness is temporary. Let's take for example someone throws you a surprise party or you buy a big house. Though you will feel very happy and excited, however in a few days, you will be over that feeling. Joy on the other hand, is lasting. It is not attached to anything happening on the outside. Isn't that amazing?! I hear you asking already, well how can I have this JOY? Well hopefully by the end of this book, I hope that question would be answered.

This book came about as a result of launching a 40 Days Joy Challenge on my Instagram page. I then desired for my siblings to partake in the challenge so I proceeded to inviting them to join via my Instagram daily posts. However, the difficulty in that is that my siblings are mostly not active on social media which they politely expressed. Thankfully, while undertaking a reoccurring act as a

Mom of 2 young kids of washing up the dishes, the idea came to turn an Instagram challenge to a book so other groups of people can have access. And here we are!

This book is written in real time. It's not just a well curated theoretically perfect piece of work. Infact this book was written at a time where the only thing that was keeping me from leaving my marriage of 4years was a command from God. I was eager to hear God tell me, 'daughter, it's time to go'. Instead, He said JOY. Joy in the midst of confusion and pain. I had to be humble to obey and this changed my outlook, my mindset, my world. It's a journey I travelled myself and strongly desired for you and the world to share in it too.

After reading this book. You will discover

- How God views joy
- Joy is your portion
- Joy is yours to have
- Joy is free and totally your choice
- Joy is God's intention for you
- Joy is paramount to productivity and creativity
- Joy is paramount to service
- Joy is totally possible in a sad cold world!

FOREWARD

The 40 Days Joy Challenge is a challenge from a Christian perspective to encourage it's readers, in a world full of struggles, heartbreak, wars, anxiety and depression, not to become comfortable living in bitterness, hate, fear, depression, jealousy and anger. Instead to be the passionate, confident, joy-filled, prosperous, **loving** and faith driven people God **intends for us to be**. The Mantra of this book is feel sad (or anger or worry or pain, etc.) but don't let sadness have you! According to Romans 14 : 17, the Bible tells us that the Kingdom of God is actually a kingdom of Joy. However, the practice starts here on earth. Psalm 144:15 (NLT) says, *"Yes, joyful are those who live like this! Joyful indeed are those whose God is the LORD'.*

I have a passion for proffering solutions. My siblings couldn't join the challenge on Instagram where it first began so I thought, 'why not turn this Instagram challenge to a book to reach many more and to impact my world with the knowledge of God's intention?' I say I thought, but really, I was prompted by God's Spirit.

Genesis 1:27-28 (KJV) gives a clear picture of God's intention when he created us. It reads. '' So God created man in his own image, **in the image of God created he him; male and female** created he them. And God blessed them, and God said unto them, **Be fruitful, and multiply, and replenish the earth, and subdue it: and have dominion** over the fish of the sea, and over the fowl of the air, and over every living thing that moveth upon the earth.''

THE 40 DAYS JOY CHALLENGE

I have put some key words in bold there as they describe, right from the mouth of God, the kind of life we all should be living! God himself lives in joy and if we are created in His image, we should too. We see this in Psalm 16:11(NKJV) which says, '" You will show me the path of life; <u>In Your presence is fullness of joy</u>; At Your right hand are pleasures forevermore ."   As God's beloved, we are not meant to live in fear, in hate, in anger and the likes; just the same way fish was not meant to live on land. We have been created to flourish in joy.

The key to attain the life that God intends for us to live is to be connected to Him.   In John 15:4-5 (NIV), Jesus speaking says, *"Remain in me, as I also remain in you. No branch can bear fruit by itself; it must remain in the vine. Neither can you bear fruit unless you remain in me. I am the vine; you are the branches. If you remain in me and I in you, you will bear much fruit; apart from me you can do nothing".* The Kinds of Fruit Jesus meant is seen in Galatians 5:22-23a (NIV) which says, " *"But the fruit of the Spirit is love, joy, peace, forbearance, kindness, goodness, faithfulness, gentleness and self-control".* A relationship with God is the source of Joy. Joy cannot be attained from external things. External things have the power to provide us happiness which is temporary. The Joy God provides is eternal. That's who He is; the eternal, immortal One. Mathew 11:25-30 (NIV) says *"Come to me, all you who are weary and burdened, and I will give you rest. Take my yoke upon you and learn from me, for I am gentle and humble of heart; and you will find rest. For my yoke is easy, and my burden is light."*

I truly pray that this book encourages you to exchange any heavy burden that is weighing you down; be it financial, relational,

xv

marital, health or any other, with the easy yoke of our Lord Jesus Christ.

THE 40 DAYS JOY CHALLENGE

DAY 1
Arise and Shine!

Introduction

I think back at when the idea to embark on a 40day Joy challenge on my Instagram page dropped in my spirit, the situations around me where not necessarily screaming JOY. I believe God was testing me in this area as well as making me living proof that JOY is a fruit of the spirit and as such not based on surrounding circumstances. Why? Because if Joy is a fruit of the Sprit and you stay connected; the spirit being God Himself, God being constant and never changing, your JOY will also be constant, never changing! Please join me on this journey, feel free to invite your friends and family as we start on this 40 day journey to a joy filled lifestyle.

Scripture

Isaiah 60:1 (NIV) - "Arise, shine, for your light has come, and the glory of the LORD rises upon you".

Commentary

You might not feel capable of shining this morning, this afternoon, this evening or whenever you get to start this devotional. However, God's word never fails; it stands for eternity and over your life,

1

THE 40 DAYS JOY CHALLENGE

calling for you to reach out and just believe and hold on to it. What better scripture to hit the road running for this 40 Day Joy Challenge than with this beautiful verse of scripture from Isaiah 60? Your time to shine is now. Your time to rejoice is now! The glory of the Lord is risen upon you. Focus on shining today. You know, most times, the things that come to steal our Joy also come to attack our shining and our lifting our heads. But God's glory is available today. I want you to memorise this verse and keep saying it to yourself until it gets so into you that YOU arise and do your best for today and shine in such a way that that thing that thought it had your joy releases that joy back to you because it's yours to have, it's yours to keep, it's your portion, it's who God made you.

Prayer

Father help me to know that you are always calling me to arise, to shine and to be all that you had in mind when you created me and I ask for grace to live this out daily through your mighty power in Jesus' name, AMEN. Help me to know that your power is available to me and that I can do all things through Christ who strengthens me in Jesus name, AMEN.

Reflections

1.How full is your joy tank today?

2.What areas of your life can you release to God today in exchange of His glory?

THE 40 DAYS JOY CHALLENGE

STUDY NOTES

DAY 2
Lean on Him

Introduction

Who made it through Day 1 in joy all day long? Heyy even if you didn't make it through the whole day long, you can choose today to make it right today through the help of God if you just lean on Him and focus your mind on the blessings and your hope of many more to come.

Scripture

Philippians 4:4 (KJV) - "Rejoice in the Lord always; and again, I say, Rejoice."

Commentary

Your joy should never be regulated or calculated by external things. God's original intention is for Him to be the source of our joy and live in joy always and He hasn't changed His mind yet. In every race, there's always a winner. In that seemingly bad condition right now, will JOY win or will depression and low self-esteem win? I pray you choose JOY.

Prayer

So Lord help me to refocus when my mind runs to my condition, thinking that there is no way out because that's a lie! There's always a way out because you are the WAY! To him that is joined to the living there is HOPE (Ecclesiastes 9 :4a). Help me to focus on this hope and rejoice in you ALWAYS in all things! Amen

Reflections

1.How can we draw joy from the source?

2.Why did God create us to live our highest versions in Joy?

THE 40 DAYS JOY CHALLENGE

STUDY NOTES

DAY 3
Surrender All; Keep Your Peace and Joy

Introduction

Let's take a bit of an inventory shall we? For me, DAY 1 was great. I was unto a great start. Then DAY 2 hit. Literally, when I say 'all hell broke loose', I mean it. It's like the enemy wanted to take every bit of joy that was left away in every way possible. I had to constantly refocus and press the reset button. I reminded God that I'm taking this walk with Him openly and with His people on my social media platforms and I couldn't default. I asked for His help as in that particular moment, I was so committed to see God truly and genuinely turn things around, give me peace in my heart so that it would not be make-up joy but true joy from Him. So, I poured out my heart to Him. I prayed earnestly and the result was pure joy that comes not from anything else but from God. Secondly, my commitment and obedience to seek out and walk in Joy in the midst of all that was going on resulted to financial increase from an unexpected source, great fellowship and healing; instant testimony of physical healing. Isn't God faithful? So, I learnt that, 1. JOY is a result. We play our part and God does the releasing. 2. The enemy is stealing from us when he causes us to live in the reality of our challenges and testing situations as opposed to surrendering them to God, keeping our peace and joy intact and walking away with a new reality. I hope my story will encourage you to really see what could be yours by just surrendering all and walking away with JOY. With 37 days more to go, we can do this.

Scripture

Luke 12:7 (KJV) - "But even the very hairs of your head are all numbered. Fear not therefore: ye are of more value than many sparrows."

Commentary

You are cared for by the Almighty. He's attention to detail concerning you is unmatchable. Children do not worry what they'll eat or how they will get from a to b. With regards to food, children just tell their parents what they want to eat; at least my daughter does. But the truth is, our father knows, He cares, He promised never to leave us nor forsake us. In the valley He's there, in the highest mountain, He's there too. In the raging storms of life, He's also there calling us to walk on water I.e. to be on top of whatever situation we are in and not the other way round and I pray today, you will take the offer.

Prayer

Father, help me to always know that you care for me, that you love me and that you're calling me higher, above my current situation. I pray for grace to walk in full knowledge of this all the days of my life that my JOY will be full as a result, in Jesus name, Amen.

Reflections

1.why do we sometimes find it difficult to obey God?

2.why do we find it difficult sometimes to surrender all to God?

STUDY NOTES

THE 40 DAYS JOY CHALLENGE

DAY 4
The Blessing of Trusting

Introduction

Welcome to Day 4. I celebrate you for making it here. Are you ready to keep going?! Your YES is more powerful than you will ever know. Please know that living a Joy-filled life doesn't mean that your life is perfect. I'm learning that being full of JOY in our world today is greatly hinged on TRUST; that God has good plans for your life no matter the pit you are in and our bible verse today really anchors on this. Shall we?

Scripture

Psalm 84:12 (NIV) - 'Lord Almighty, blessed is the one who trusts in you'.

Commentary

Wow! I think we could all do with reading this verse everyday as a reminder that our trust in God, even in a bad situation is translating to blessings! Trusting in God means not fully holding on to the doctor's negative report, not relying on the not-so encouraging statistics, not trusting on what the economy looks like or even our sometimes negative thoughts. Trusting in God means holding on to what He says and nothing else!

Prayer

Father help me to place my trust in you always and not be moved. Cause me to recognise and see the blessings that follow from trusting you, in Jesus name I pray, Amen

Reflections

1.What does it mean to trust God?

2. What actions can you take today to let God know that you fully trust in Him?

THE 40 DAYS JOY CHALLENGE

STUDY NOTES

THE 40 DAYS JOY CHALLENGE

DAY 5
Inexpressible and Glorious Joy!

Introduction

I'm so thankful for what is being produced in us through this challenge. A life of possibilities, intentionality and most especially, JOY which really is an essential part of our make-up in order for us to really experience and exhaust all that we have the potentials to, here on earth. If you're fighting for your JOY intentionally with me in this season, I want to say congratulations and by the grace of God, by the time we arrive at Day 40, being Joyful will become a natural part of you.

Scripture

1 Peter 1:8 (NIV) - "Though you have not seen him you love him; and even though you do not see him now, you believe in him and are filled with an inexpressible and glorious joy"

Commentary

God is the source of JOY. When you love Him with all your heart, all your soul and all your might, He pours out JOY to you as a reward. With our own strength and efforts, we couldn't really have joy. There are so many difficulties, disappointments and heartbreaks in our world today constantly attacking our sound mind and joy. However, through loving God, Joy is released to us even in the midst of our situations; and enough that it overflows to the people around us.

Prayer

So help us Lord to Love you in the midst of unpleasant situations; that your Joy will be released and remain in our hearts forever. We pray that our lives would be filled and overflowing with the power of God's love so we can make a difference in this world and bring honor to God. We ask for your help in reminding us that the most important things are not what we do outwardly, not our talents or gifts, not possessions or pursuit of things but the most significant thing we can do in this life is simply to love you Lord and to choose to love others according to your word in 1 Corinthians 13. So, help us Lord, in Jesus's name, Amen.

Reflections

1.What does it mean to love God?

2.How can you show God today that you love Him?

THE 40 DAYS JOY CHALLENGE

STUDY NOTES

DAY 6
Sing For Joy!

Introduction

Wow God is being glorified! Are you being changed? Please let me know via the mediums I share at the end of this book. I really want growth for you, to be ALL that God had in mind when He created you and one of those intentions is for your JOY to be Full. Anxiety and stress, pain and worry are not your identity. Wrong self-image and shame are not your portion. God is the ultimate manufacturer and in you He has placed all of His Glory. According to Isaiah 60:1, you are worthy of God's glory.

Scripture

Isaiah 12:6 (NIV) - "Shout aloud and sing for joy, people of Zion, for great is the Holy One of Israel among you."

Commentary

In Day 5, we said to Love God is to have JOY. But how can you love who you don't even know about? Is God among you? If He is, then it's so easy to shout for JOY because you KNOW the Great one who is among you and for you. If you want to know God, please pray the below prayer with me:

Prayer

I want to really know you God. Come fill my heart. Teach me. Help me. Change my heart to be for you. Let your Spirit come and live on the inside of me. I repent and I turn to you today, help me to live all the days of my life in ways pleasing to you and bringing glory to your holy name, in Jesus's name, Amen!- (If you prayed this prayer, celebrate, read his word online/physical bible, plug to a Christian church or friendship, find ways to grow your faith and I pray you see the mighty works of God in your life too)

Reflections

1. What does it mean to have a relationship with God?
2. How can one cultivate a true lasting relationship?

THE 40 DAYS JOY CHALLENGE

STUDY NOTES

THE 40 DAYS JOY CHALLENGE

DAY 7
You Are Valuable

Introduction

It's Day 7! Today we are focusing on self-love as a key factor in living a joy-filled life! You are special. You are amazing. You are Beautiful. You are worth every good thing the earth has to offer because you were bought with a special price; the blood of Jesus! So often we base our value by what people think about us, how successful we are, how perfect of a life we live. The problem with all of these is that they are subject to change. Your value should be based solely on the basis that you are a child of God! Ready for the Bible verse of the day?

Scripture

Ephesians 2:10 (NKJV) "For we are his workmanship, created in Christ Jesus for good works, which God prepared beforehand that we should walk in them"

Commentary

Do you know that YOU are God's marvelous handwork; well crafted, designed, created for ONLY good works? You are loved! You didn't just appear on earth for no reason. There is a specific purpose for why you are here; for GOOD WORKS says the word of God! God breathed his life into you. You have the DNA of the Almighty God. However, what we find in our society and our generation is the invitation to look outside to determine self-worth and the level of self-love; for women, your weight size and make-up, for men, your bank account, the car you drive, house you live, your profession or title. But nothing we do can make us any more valuable. You are valuable right now. God calls you a masterpiece. By the power in the name of Jesus, I believe this book will be as a tool, cutting down any ideologies and perceptions attacking your self-love, self-worth and ultimately your Joy. Celebrate YOU!; just as you are, in all your glorious strengths and weaknesses, talents and quirks, wins and mistakes because you are deeply loved by the Father.

Prayer

Oh Father, thank you Lord that I am a daughter/son of a king loved and cherished, and my inheritance is eternal goodness. Today I wear my crown like a princess/prince that I truly am. Every other crown I let go of right now in this moment. Full of humility, for I do not earn this honour, I simply choose to live in it from today. I place this price upon my head and by the power of your word, nothing outside of this knowledge will influence my thoughts and emotions. I ask for your grace dear Lord within my heart not to fear failure, grace that calls me to stay true to my values and visions, but not to be overwhelmed by them. Grace to walk tall, following in your footsteps. Thank you, Lord, for I am your jewel, completely inestimable and I walk in this reality all the days of my life, in Jesus' name, Amen

Reflections

1. What does self-love/self-worth mean to you?
2. 2.Why is it difficult sometimes not to fall under the pressure of society to fit in in order to feel important?
3. 3.Why is it important not to base our value on things, titles and people?

STUDY NOTES

THE 40 DAYS JOY CHALLENGE

THE 40 DAYS JOY CHALLENGE

DAY 8
Ask and You Will Receive

Introduction

Welcome to Day 8. We are making progress. Before you know it, JOY will become a habit and a way of life which is one of the key objectives for this 40 Days Joy Challenge.

As much as I believe that there are really grim situations out there, truly devastating, horrific and heart braking. You might be reading this and thinking, yes, I've been through situations like that. First of all, You went THROUGH. Can we take a two minutes hallelujah praise break?! Secondly, I also believe God's word. I believe It's true (through FAITH) and I've tested and proved it for myself. God's Word tells me that He, (Jesus) came so I can have life and life in abundance. Abundant life sounds like a JOY-filled life to me; not because everything is perfect but because you know who your God is and in who you have placed your trust. I choose to hold on to what God says about me day by day and not what my current circumstance wants me to believe because that's temporary. I choose to hold on to that which is EVERLASTING, and that's the Word of God!

25

THE 40 DAYS JOY CHALLENGE

Scripture

John 16:24 (NIV) - "Until now you have not asked for anything in my name. Ask and you will receive, and your joy will be complete"

Commentary

Have you prayed about what makes you worried? There's nothing that brings JOY like answered prayer. God in our verse for today is appealing to us saying, *we've not asked Him in His name*! I want to ask you, what is the first thing you do when faced with a difficult situation? Do you go to people first or do you ask God? I have a detailed video on *how to pray effectively* on my YouTube Channel - AmakaToby TV. I will encourage you to head over and watch the full video and I pray that as you pray to God today over those situations you want a positive change, I pray you receive the answer speedily and that your joy will be full! Let's pray.

Prayer

Dear heavenly Father, I completely surrender my life to you. From my past to my present, all that I am I give to you because I know you are the God who can turn my disappointments, my pains, my failures into a glorious testimony. Whatever that has ever caused me pain, shame and disappointment, I ask for a celebration over that same thing. Let your name be glorified over my life, in Jesus's name, Amen!

Reflections

1. Who do you talk to first when you are faced with a challenging situation?
2. How often do you go to God in prayer?
3. What mechanism can you put in place today to improve your prayer life?

STUDY NOTES

THE 40 DAYS JOY CHALLENGE

THE 40 DAYS JOY CHALLENGE

DAY 9
Stay Thankful

Introduction

Day 9! You made it. JOY is about to be a way of life for you. Can I hear an Amen? It's been proven that the more we repeatedly do a thing, the more that thing becomes a habit. I once heard it said that " *Excellence is not an act, but a habit"*. The same applies to joy. I believe this is why God wanted this challenge to be for 40 Days. To change anxiety, worry, anger, discouragements and bitterness, we must repeatedly choose joy, love, peace and faith. There is guaranteed change if you truly walk this challenge seriously, being open to God's light and revelation! All ready?

Scripture

Psalm 9:1 (NIV) - "I will give thanks to you, LORD, with all my heart; I will tell of all your wonderful deeds."

Commentary

One of the key ways to experience JOY is through THANKFULNESS. When your whole heart is filled with thanks to God, there wouldn't be any place or space left for anxiety, worry, depression and all other negative emotions. The result would be a

29

THE 40 DAYS JOY CHALLENGE

joyful heart. Being thankful for the simple little things we often overlook is one of the easiest ways to experience Joy. A wiseman once said that when we give thanks, we are applying to God for more. I remember the story of the 10 lepers in the Bible that were healed by Jesus. Only one out of the 10 came back to say thank you to Jesus and for that reason, he received a greater portion than the 9. There is a greater portion available to you on the other side of your thankfulness.

Often, we focus on the things we don't have when we can have it all by just thanking God for what we do have. I pray that from today, you will not overlook this powerful key to experiencing real joy. I pray that you will be thankful for the little things and in the little things. Let's all find at least ONE reason to be thankful to God today. Even better, every morning as we wake, let our first words be words of thankfulness to God.

Prayer

Heavenly Father, thank you for your love. Thank you for the gifts you so freely give us; even when we take them for granted. Thank you that I'm alive reading this book. Thank you that I can breathe, that I have a roof over my head, that you've always provided, that you've never left me without a way. I just give you thanks Lord today for all that you are, for all that you've done and for all that you have planned for me, in Jesus name, Amen

Reflections

1. 1.How often do you give total thanks to God?
2. 2.What can you give God thanks for today? LIST ATLEAST 7 THINGS!
3. 3.Comit to thanking God daily for the little day by day miracles like waking up from sleep

THE 40 DAYS JOY CHALLENGE

STUDY NOTES

DAY 10
The Value of God's Promises

Introduction

Welcome to Day 10! 30days to go. How is your inside looking? If you've been following this challenge seriously, I want you to look within and honestly answer that question.

Scripture

Psalm 119:162 (NIV) - "I rejoice in your promise like one who finds great spoil".

Commentary

The value of God's promises are beyond measure! They are literally TREASURES hidden in the pages of our Bibles. Sadly, many of us today do not know or live out the promises of God for us. God gave us His promises so that we can have them in our hearts and be JOYFUL in them knowing that it is true and that is our inheritance! Some of God's promises include the promise that God never changes (Hebrews 13:8), the promise of impossibilities becoming possible (Matthew 19:26) , the promise of victory (1 Corinthians 15:57) and finally, the promise of the Holy Spirit (Romans 5:5). I pray that each day, you will search out at least one promise of God from the pages of your Bible for yourself and hide it in your heart for a victorious Day!

Prayer

Dear Heavenly Father, I pray for the urge and burning desire to daily search out the treasure chest of your promises for me. That I may live an abundant life through the knowledge of your word (the Bible); that my JOY will be FULL as I do, in Jesus' name, Amen.

Reflections

1. Have you searched out God's promise over your life?
2. What actions do you take daily in line with that promise?

THE 40 DAYS JOY CHALLENGE

STUDY NOTES

THE 40 DAYS JOY CHALLENGE

DAY 11
A Merry Heart Doeth Good

Introduction

Welcome to Day 11. I must confess that it hasn't been a walk in the park for me to keep my JOY full in this season. However, that's not surprising. Whenever we decide to embark on anything transformational or take a stand for God, there will be hindrances, temptations and oppositions. In 1 Corinthians 16:9, .the Bible says, *'because a great door for effective work has opened to me, and there are many who oppose me'*. Don't allow the opposition stop you. Long story cut short, if you are truly aligned with God, the end result is predictable, shouts of JOY and VICTORY! Take a two minutes Hallelujah praise break if you believe that will be your testimony too!

Scripture

Proverbs 17:22 (KJV) - "A merry heart doeth good like a medicine: but a broken spirit drieth the bones"

Commentary

Even for those who do not wholly believe the Bible, it's been scientifically and medically proven that LAUGHTER is STRONG MEDICINE, just like the Bible rightly says. According to research, laughter triggers healthy physical and emotional balances in the body. Laughter strengthens the immune system, diminishes pain and depression and protects from stress. It's the cheapest medicine there is. Like the verse for today says, a broken spirit i.e one who is without much laughter dries up the bones! That is not our portion. Your laughter is a victory sound in the camp of the enemy. Do not allow that situation, that is subject to change, rob you of this free yet powerful medicine in laughter.

Prayer

Whatever it is that wants to keep me from laughing today and every day of my life, I release power in the name of Jesus at that thing. My joy will be full and my body, mind and soul will be healed and remain in good health, in Jesus' name, Amen!

Reflections

1. 1.How easy has it been for you to keep your joy up until now?
2. 2.How have you been able to combat the things that have tried to attack and steal your joy in this journey to a JOY

FILLED LIFE!

3. 3.How many times have you laughed out today? (3 times or more is the target as we generally eat 3 times a day!)

STUDY NOTES

THE 40 DAYS JOY CHALLENGE

DAY 12
Testimony Amidst The Storms

Introduction

Have you followed the challenge daily so far? If not, I will like to invite you to read-up on the days you have missed, commit to the 40 Days Joy Challenge and consciously take steps to keep your JOY. That's literally it! I share daily notes and Bible verses to spur us on each day on our journey.

The aim of this challenge, as well as providing a practical insightful tool, is to make us equipped and better people to handle the challenges of life and not be drowned in them; to have a testimony even amidst the storms and this is totally possible. This is my testimony. One single starting principle can be found in Philippians 4:6-7. A lack of peace is a lack of Joy. However, what our Heavenly Father is eager to deliver to us is that peace that doesn't make sense and I pray we will release ourselves to receive that today.

Joy comes from God (the source) as we've already learnt. However, we have a part to play. Once you play that part, you can hands-off and watch God do His Mighty Part. The biggest part we have to play is what we are looking at in our verse for today. Ready?

Scripture

Psalm 119:47 (KJV) - "And I will delight myself in thy commandments, which I have loved."

Commentary

To delight in God's commandments is to OBEY them. Obedience to God's instructions brings Joy and Blessings! I'm reminded by many persons in the Bible who rejoiced as a result of obeying God's commands; Nehemiah, David, Abraham, Joshua. Many of us KNOW God's commands but choose the ones we like and the ones we don't like . This is not the Christianity that produces great and mighty results like the God we serve! Some on the other hand simply do not live and delight in God's commandments. In Day 3, I shared my personal testimonies as a result of me being committed to obeying God's commands. The benefits are for us, not God. They are not just God's restrictions to make us have miserable lives, no.

Let's look at Joshua 1:8 (NIV), God said this to Joshua, " Keep this Book of Law always on your lips; meditate on it day and night, so that you may be careful to do everything written in it. Then you will be prosperous and successful ". Being careful to obey God's word brings success which in turn leads to a joy-filled heart and life. God's ultimate plan for us is JOY. I pray this challenge will set you in motion to keep your JOY full always by practicing the tools revealed in this challenge in order to be productive, free and live out the full potentials that are down on the inside of you, Amen.

Prayer

Father God, Thou art the only true God and Thou art the only wise God. Wiser than the wisest, bigger than the biggest yet condescends to love His people as a father. Help us, O God, to be obedient children, to every word you have given us. Help us also to cast out of our hearts and minds all things that might hinder us in a whole and holy love for Thee, that we, by doing so will make our own ways prosperous and enjoy a JOY-FILLED Life, in Jesus's name we pray, Amen!.

Reflections

1. What is the purpose of God's laws?
2. Why do we find it difficult to obey God's commandments sometimes?

THE 40 DAYS JOY CHALLENGE

STUDY NOTES

THE 40 DAYS JOY CHALLENGE

DAY 13
The Secret of Being Content

Introduction

Welcome to Day 13. My prayer is that so far, you have been impacted with the knowledge and the power of JOY and that it is bearing fruit in your day to day life.

Scripture

Philippians 4 :12b-13 (NIV) - " I have learned the secret of being content in any and every situation, whether well fed or hungry, whether living in plenty or in want. I can do all things through Him who gives me strength".

Commentary

This verse reveals that there is in fact a way to be content, regardless of your current situation. In a World where so many of us are trying to fill a void of some kind in our lives with things that can't actually satisfy, receiving the word 'CONTENTMENT' this morning from the Holy Spirit as one of the keys to a joyful heart had to be just right!

When you focus on God as your source; the One who makes ALL THINGS possible for you, you will have contentment in your situation. Being content doesn't mean settling, lowering your standards or accepting any and everything, no. Being content is simply appreciating where you are and what you have while working towards what you want. You have a dream doesn't mean you can't be grateful for now? The truth of the matter is that you are blessed!; regardless of your state! The difficulty sometimes is when we occupy our minds with what we want and the better we desire for our lives, forgetting to be thankful for the present, for the opportunity of a new day. Stay in peace. God is the door keeper. He is the Way and at the right time, he opens the right doors.

Prayer

Father Lord help me to recognise my blessings and thank you every day for them. Help me not to be bitter over things I don't have yet because I know in due time, I will have them all; because you are a good father. Help me to celebrate with others that do have the things I'm praying for; in Jesus name, Amen.

Reflection

1. 1.What does contentment mean to you?
2. 2.How can you balance between contentment and pursuing your dreams and desires?

STUDY NOTES

DAY 14
The Recipe For Thoughts

Introduction

Welcome to Day 14! Do you know your thoughts are your mood thermostat? Do you know your thoughts determine your decisions and your decisions your actions? Your thoughts can literally lead you to the life you desire or away from it. What are you thinking today?

Today's verse is what I like to call our *Recipe For Thinking*, perfectly curated by God Himself, the Author and Finisher, the Master Potter. If only we can follow the recipe, we ourselves will become a well-cooked sumptuous and attractive meal. Ready for day 14?

Scripture

Philippians 4:8 (NIV) - "Finally, brothers and sisters, whatever is true, whatever is noble, whatever is right, whatever is pure, whatever is lovely, whatever is admirable- if anything is excellent or praiseworthy- think about such things".

Commentary

There's nothing more to add to our reading for today. If we can consciously regulate our thoughts in line with the recipe above, there is no doubt that we will be joyful. There will not be room for bitterness, depression, addiction, jealousy, suicidal thoughts, envy or not enough mentality; a life of JOY will be the end result!

Prayer

So, Father help me to think only thoughts that align with Philippians 4:8 every day and let it be seen through my interactions with the people around me; so that my JOY will be FULL always, in Jesus name, Amen

Reflections

1. 1.How do you consciously regulate your thoughts?
2. 2.What measures do you have in place to keep your thoughts in line with the reading for today? (open floor for open discussion if in group discussion)

THE 40 DAYS JOY CHALLENGE

STUDY NOTES

THE 40 DAYS JOY CHALLENGE

DAY 15
The Path of Life

Introduction

We literally have 25 more days to go! What a work out! Who still wants to keep going? I hope you do; for your health, for your family, for your community, for our nations! Our emotional state affects everything including our physical body. When you are nervous for example, you may notice your face flushes, heart races or even an increase in body temperature causing sweating. Have you ever stopped to wonder how much more is happening internally (heart, lungs, muscles, etc.) that we don't get to see when we harbour negative emotions?! So, here is my solution, a challenge for 40 days and hopefully beyond, to cultivate a lifestyle of JOY, peace and thankfulness.

Scripture

Psalm 16:11 (NIV) - "You make known to me the path of life; you will fill me with joy in your presence, with eternal pleasures at your right hand".

Commentary

I love God's presence. It's stress free, I can be myself, it's peaceful, its humbling, its filled with glory, Joy, love, wisdom and pleasures unimaginable. You want wisdom? Get in His presence. You want to know the path of life? Get in God's presence. In a world where we are all too busy 'getting' things, I want to encourage us to make out time to spend in his presence, to renew our strength and most especially, our JOY. It may be a sacrifice sometimes to make out time which is why it's called 'spending' time but it is time worth every spend.

Prayer

Dear Heavenly Father, I ask for discipline to cultivate quiet regular time with you, a relationship that nothing can take away from; knowledge of the path of life; that I will be filled with JOY and eternal pleasures all the days of my life, in Jesus's name, Amen.

Reflections

1. 1.How do you think your internal organs react to negative emotions like worry, bitterness, anxiety, etc?
2. 2.What will you put in place to create regular quiet time with God?

STUDY NOTES

THE 40 DAYS JOY CHALLENGE

THE 40 DAYS JOY CHALLENGE

DAY 16
Get Some Rest

Introduction

Hi There! I'm elated to see you back on Day 16! In today's challenge, we are dealing with something so relevant and common. If you are a Mother, most especially with young kids, you will totally understand the need for today's challenge.

Scripture

Mark 6:31 (NIV) - "Then, because so many people were coming and going that they did not even have a chance to eat, he said to them, "Come with me by yourselves to a quiet place and get some rest".

Commentary

I would love to dedicate today's challenge to all mothers; especially my own mother who had 5 of us. Being a Mama myself, I know it is exhausting. It's a job role that requires all of you and some more. As if that is not enough, some of us feel guilty when we get to rest. Dear Mum, that is a lie of the devil! God cares for us and believes REST is important and encourages it. Many verses in the Bible tell us about the importance of rest, is just like our verse for today.

When we ignore rest, we get burnt out, quick tempered, make bad decisions and the list goes on! If you're a Mama following this challenge, I want to encourage you to seek out time for yourself and honour the need for rest.

Prayer

Dear Heavenly Father, I ask for the discipline and faith to get rest when I need to; setting my hearts at rest in you. For your word says, whoever dwells in you shall find rest in you. Thank you Lord that you desire that we will be full of strength and not overburdened. Help us to consciously cast our cares on you and rest light hearted, knowing that that we rest in the mighty arms of the Almighty, who is at the same time, mixing and positioning every of our life events to favour us. Thank you, Lord in Jesus name, Amen.

Reflections

1. Do you believe at the moment that you have a healthy work- rest balance?
2. How will you change your schedule to incorporate more rest?

THE 40 DAYS JOY CHALLENGE

STUDY NOTES

DAY 17
You Are Greater

Introduction

Can I take a moment to testify to the glory of God. This challenge has changed my thinking, my home, my relationships, my identity in Christ. I pray it's changing you too, your surrounding and your relationships.

I didn't really have the blue print before embarking on this journey. Certainly, I didn't foresee all the goodness behind this challenge. However, I have found out again, that God's plans and intentions for ALL of us is for joy because He's just a good Father. He will equip where He calls and He is Faithful to do exceedingly, abundantly, above all we can think or imagine.

Scripture

1 John 4:4 (NIV) -"You, dear children, are from God and have overcome them, because the one who is in you is greater than the one who is in the world".

Commentary

Do you truly know who you are in Christ? Do you know you are the head and not the tail? Do you know you are on top only and not beneath? (Deuteronomy 28 :13). The Bible reveals to us wonderful truths about our real identity; some which are contrary to what our experiences, our present and even the world system tells us. Knowing your identity in Christ provokes actions in line with that nature; part of which is a joyful experience of life. Why? Because our faith is in God, He lives in us and He has commanded us to be anxious for nothing! Our text for today calls us overcomers! That is our true identity and I pray we walk in this from today on.

Prayer

Dear Heavenly Father cause my eyes to be opened to see myself right in the light of your intention when you put me in my mother's womb. That I will truly understand that it is my heritage to experience a JOY-Filled life all the days of my life, in Jesus's name, Amen.

Reflections

1. How has this challenge changed how you view yourself?
2. How has this challenge changed your surrounding and environment?
3. How has this challenge changed your relationships?

THE 40 DAYS JOY CHALLENGE

STUDY NOTES

THE 40 DAYS JOY CHALLENGE

DAY 18
Meditate on His Word

Introduction

How is your journey to a joy-filled life so far? Have you been consciously practicing all of the practical tools this book provides? It only takes a decision by the help of the Holy Spirit to decide to allow joy to become your mood thermostat. Now that you have done that, let's look at our key text for today.

Scripture

John 15:11 (NIV) - "I have told you this so that my joy may be in you and that your joy may be complete".

Commentary

Reading God's word daily and knowing what God said is essential to living a joy-filled life. How often do you meditate on His Word? If not daily, I want this to be a reminder to encourage you to cultivate a daily habit of reading and meditating on God's Word. His word is nourishment that cannot be found anywhere else. Jeremiah 15: 16a (NIV) says, 'When *your words came, I ate them; they were my joy and my heart's delight* '. God's word is our joy meal. It's our reset button/navigation when we find ourselves drifting towards and into the storms in our lives.

Prayer

So, help us Father to be disciplined to make out time daily to search and meditate on your Word; that through your Word, we will acquire the full armour of God to enable us live out a joy-filled and victorious life, in Jesus name, Amen

Reflections

1. 1.How regularly do you read and meditate on God's Word?
2. 2.What can you do differently to free up time to read your Bible more often?

THE 40 DAYS JOY CHALLENGE

STUDY NOTES

DAY 19
Celebrate!

Introduction

It's God's desire that we do not lack testimonies and celebrations. It's God's pleasure to see us filled with Joy. If you are reading this and you do not believe in celebration or that there is any need to, my prayer is that your understanding is changed and refreshed through the knowledge you will receive from today's challenge.

Scripture

Nehemiah 8:10 (NIV) - "Nehemiah said, "Go and enjoy choice food and sweet drinks, and send some to those who have nothing prepared. This day is holy to our Lord. Do not grieve, for the joy of the Lord is your strength".

Commentary

To celebrate is to rejoice! Celebration dissolves grief. Celebration is an expression of thanks and like we already looked at in this challenge, thankfulness is key in order to live out a joy-filled life! Celebration goes the extra mile in comparison to thanksgiving in that in most cases, it involves food, drinks, and people. Who can deny the power of good food? The truth is that God wants shouts of joy to be continually heard from our lips. Another resounding truth is that if we honestly search within, we will find reasons to celebrate the graciousness of our God. How often do you celebrate God's mercies and loving- kindness towards you? As you celebrate God and even in the littlest provisions, I pray He blows your mind in a thousand ways in Jesus name, Amen!

Prayer

Dear Heavenly Father, I apologise for the ways I have been ungrateful and not celebrated your loving-kindness towards me. I ask for your mercy. Please forgive me. From today, I choose to celebrate, even in the little things of life to the glory of your name. Thank you, Lord, in Jesus name, Amen.

Reflections

1. When was the last time you went out of your way to truly celebrate yourself, God's mercies or an event?
2. Think of ways to incorporate more celebration into your life. (they don't have to be very big celebrations either)

THE 40 DAYS JOY CHALLENGE

STUDY NOTES

DAY 20
There Is A Reward!

Introduction

First of all, I pray a blessing over you today as you read the challenge for today. May lines fall in pleasant places FOR YOU, in Jesus's name, Amen!

You know writing this book is simply God showing off on His faithfulness. I'm sure His eager to show off in your life too. Each day, I simply depend on Him to release the word for the day's challenge. At some point it felt impossible to complete a whole 40 Day journey. I started thinking of ways to help God. I tried to prepare the challenge a day before but the Holy Spirt made it clear that I must wait on Him in each new day to release the challenge of the day. No pressure Lord. But just like the Israelites in the desert, God provided. Little wonder He encourages us to live our lives day by day and not to 'worry' about tomorrow. How difficult that is sometimes for us to do, which often is the root of stress, anxiety, depression and indeed some illnesses. However, the good news is, today we can hand over our concerns, pains, worries, uncertainties to the One who has the power to bring about change. The One whose shoulders are big enough to carry

THE 40 DAYS JOY CHALLENGE

whatever is causing us stress and so much worry, so that we can truly find rest in JOY. His burden is easy and His yoke is light. Say no today, to picking that worry back up, that insecurity, that thought that tells you that there will never be change, that your life will not turn for the better and live free with the Joy of the Lord that nothing can take away. So then day 20, let's get to it.

Scripture

2 Chronicles 15:7 (NIV)- "But as for you, be strong and do not give up, for your work will be rewarded".

Commentary

One way God rewards us is through the joy He gives. In today's verse, God is encouraging us not to give up on our work. God is aware that sometimes, we may feel weak. Sometimes we may be putting so much energy in something and yet we don't see the change we desire. It could be our work, marriage, friendship, health, children, finance, you name it. But today, God is saying, do not give up my son. Do not give up my daughter. Do not give up my child. There is a reward. The Bible tells us not to be weary in well doing. Even when it's difficult to extend love, peace to someone who may not deserve it, God says, do not give up on doing good. There is a reward on the other side of your good work. Do not allow the enemy steal that reward from you through anger, reaction, bitterness, depression or the likes. Get up, be strong and keep doing good.

Another aspect of this verse is the mention of 'your work'. Our work here at the core refers to God's purpose over our lives. His calling, the reason why we are still alive. NOTE, that it did not say *job*. There is a difference that only you can bring to the world! We can name many great historians who made a difference such as Nelson Mandela and Martin Luther King Jr.

The Bible in Mathew Chapter 5 :14 calls us *Light*. It went ahead to say that we are a city set on a hill that cannot be hidden. What talent, gifts are inside of you right now that are still hidden? The purpose of light is to shine and to relieve anyone around it of darkness. Your WORK is your light. Your work is what will bring fulfilment to your life and that is God's will for you! Have you discovered God's purpose for you? Have you given up on that purpose? Nobody says it will be easy to chase purpose and that's why we are encouraged not to give up. However, what is certain is the reward, the fulfillment and guaranteed joy because we would be functioning in line with the Manufacturer's (God) manual.

Prayer

So Heavenly Father, reveal my purpose to me, my work. Make it plain and clear and give me the confidence to pursue it; that I will gain that wonderful reward you have promised and shine as light in my world, in Jesus name, Amen (Bonus: This makes for a good daily prayer until God fully reveals His purpose for you).

Reflections

1. 1.Have you discovered your work; God's purpose for your life?

2. 2.What are you doing now to pursue or bring your purpose into full action?

3. 3.What talent(s) / gift(s) are you utilising to be a blessing and to shine as light for your world?

THE 40 DAYS JOY CHALLENGE

STUDY NOTES

DAY 21
Be Good To People

Introduction

My desire is that this challenge is helpful, is a blessing and it brings about positive change in your heart, your family and in every facet of your life. I pray as you make it to the end, you will never lack reasons to rejoice in Jesus name, Amen!

Scripture

2 Thessalonians 3:13 (NIV) - "And as for you, brothers and sisters, never tire of doing what is good"

Commentary

Doing good and reaching out to be a blessing to another is a sure way to experience joy. Sometimes we can get so fixated in our own struggles and battles that we miss the opportunity to receive joy, simply by stepping out and being a blessing to someone else. Other times, we allow our experiences or past hurts stop us from believing that doing good pays. Well, Hebrews 6:10 (NIV) says this - "*God is not unjust; he will not forget your work and the love you have shown him as you have helped his people and continue to help them*." God does not forget. He is a MIGHTY REWARDER. Therefore, in today's challenge, I'm encouraging us to extend kindness to someone today; reach out in love and be a blessing today and as you do, I pray your reward is not delayed in Jesus name, Amen!

Prayer

Most gracious Father, we thank you for choosing us even when we did not choose you. Thank you that your mercies are new every morning. Give us the grace to be the smile of God to the people you send our way. Help us not to measure how we help others by how they treat us or through the lens of our struggles. But that we will share your love always, in Jesus' name, Amen.

Reflections

1. 1.When was the last time you extended help to someone else?

2. 2.In what way can you be a blessing today to someone else?

THE 40 DAYS JOY CHALLENGE

STUDY NOTES

THE 40 DAYS JOY CHALLENGE

DAY 22
Forgive Them

Introduction

Welcome to Day 22. Today we are looking at unforgiveness and how it really hinders joy. I heard a saying once that unforgiveness is like taking pain killers for someone else's headache and expecting the headache to leave. It doesn't work that way right? Unforgiveness is bearing a weight that is not yours and has been proven to cause mental disorders and sicknesses. We might not necessarily see the effects of unforgiveness physically but that doesn't change the fact that the effects are there. Therefore, as we walk into the new year, let us be intentional to walk in WHOLE, FREE, SPIRIT-FILLED and JOY FILLED, Amen.

Scripture

Mark 11:25 (NIV) - "And when you stand praying, if you hold anything against anyone, forgive them, so that your Father in heaven may forgive you your sins."

Commentary

FORGIVENESS is a key part of our walk with God. Without forgiveness, we cannot say we have a working relationship with the Father (God). It's almost like saying, *I love God but I don't have a heart for people.* It doesn't work well right?

Like I mentioned, we can't say we have a working relationship with God if we don't practice forgiveness. Forgiveness is an integral part of our relationship with God because offenses will come. The Bible assures us of this fact. According to Luke 17:1a, *"Jesus said to his disciples: "Things that cause people to stumble are bound to come ".* However, we are not at the mercies of offences. We combat the effects of offences by the help of the Holy Spirit through forgiveness and in turn enjoy a joy-filled experience of life! It might not be easy at first to forgive a hurtful situation; however, the knowledge that holding a grudge is like taking pain killers for someone else's headache, will hopefully aid the process. When we hold a grudge, we release the power over our emotions to that person. I want to encourage you to take your power back today and forgive.

Of course, we ourselves will also need forgiving as we are not perfect and for God to forgive us, we must forgive the ones that have offended us. We must release the ones who have hurt us from the grip of unforgiveness, hatred, malice, anger and every type of bitterness for God to fill that space with something much more beautiful, attractive and chain breaking; JOY.

Prayer

Father, today we pray for grace and a soft heart not to seek to avenge our offenders ourselves but to offer forgiveness because truthfully, you will deliver better judgment that we would. More of you and less of us we pray, in Jesus name, Amen.

Reflections

1. 1.Why do you think is hard for us sometimes to overlook offences?
2. 2.How easy is it for you to forgive offences?
3. 3.What principle can you put in place to counter the effects of an offence towards you?

THE 40 DAYS JOY CHALLENGE

STUDY NOTES

THE 40 DAYS JOY CHALLENGE

DAY 23
The Hand of God

Introduction

1 7 days to go. This is a work out like no other! But thank God we're not left to it by our strength because by strength shall no man prevail (1 Samuel 2: 9c).

Would you like to experience deep and enduring joy? Would you like to be joyful? Be assured that it is possible, and you can and my hope with this challenge is to show you through God's Word that it is both God's intention for you and that you can have it. Let's jump right into it.

In a world where there is woeful shortage of joy and a surplus of fear, discouragement, worry, tension and depression, pursuit for "happiness", I pray this challenge brings understanding and light to you to live this life burden free and truly joyful.

Scripture

Psalm 126:2 (NIV)- 'Our mouths were filled with laughter, our tongues with songs of joy. Then it was said among the nations, "The

Lord has done great things for them."

Commentary

According to our Bible text for today, Joy is an evidence that God's hand is upon a person's life to bring about great miracles. What is the difference between HAPPINESS and JOY? Well, happiness is an emotion and like most emotions, it is temporary. Ecclesiastes 3:4 (NIV) says, *"There is a time to weep, and a time to laugh; a time to mourn, and a time to dance"*- could you imagine counting on just happiness during mourning season?

What is joy? First of all, joy comes from filling the spiritual void inside of each of us primarily with an intimate relationship with the One who is pure JOY Himself. Jesus puts it this way in John 15:5 (NKJV) - "I *am the vine, you are the branches. He who abides in Me, and I in him bears much fruit"*. According to Galatians 5:22, that FRUIT includes JOY. Note also that JOY is the second on the list of the fruits of the Spirit. This indicates how important Joy actually is as followers of Christ.

We often fall into the danger of pursuing happiness by getting things; buying that handbag, car, shoes, food, even getting married, pursuing career. However, *THINGS* can only provide a temporary feeling of happiness. JOY is that which comes from the inside, from the depth of your relationship with God. And I pray that we will walk consciously in this, not pursuing happiness but JOY which ultimately is a gift of the Spirit and that we will continuously abide in God; our

safe place, that our JOY will be full even in challenging times, Amen!

Prayer

So, Father God we ask for grace to walk consciously in this, not pursuing happiness but joy which ultimately is a gift of the Spirit and that we will continuously abide in you; our safe place, that our JOY will be full at all times, in Jesus name, Amen!

Reflections

1. 1.What does joy look like to you?
2. 2.What is one way that you cultivate joy in your life?

THE 40 DAYS JOY CHALLENGE

STUDY NOTES

DAY 24
Commit It To The Lord

Introduction

Welcome to Day 24. I'm so thankful to God to have made it this far on this challenge and that you have made it too. It has literally been by God's help and has been life changing to walk this journey. I hope that so far, its transformational for you also.

A lot of us underestimate the power of JOY or don't even know how key it is in order to achieve our assignment on earth. Nothing created is without purpose and a wise man once said that, *where purpsose is unknown, abuse is inevitable.*

Joy is strength. Joy is wisdom. Joy is breakthrough. Joy is victory. Joy is abundance. Joy is speed. Joy is self-esteem. Joy is the essence of life. Little wonder the Christmas season is announced with the words, 'Joy to the World'. I truly invite you, you want to see change? Don't take this challenge or joy in your heart lightly, IT WILL CHANGE YOUR LIFE!

Scripture

Proverbs 16:3 (NIV) - "Commit to the Lord whatever you do and he will establish your plans".

Commentary

Note our verse for today says *plans*. God can handle all of our plans including the ones we cannot see right now, how they can be manifested. And when God establishes your plans, there will be nothing else but shouts of JOY! Our verse today simply tells us that joy is the reward when we do our part which is not carrying the burdens of our plans: but instead committing our desires to the one who is able to do exceedingly, the Alpha and the Omega.

Another great thing about setting out a plan in the first place, is that it combats time wasting. There is nothing that sucks joy like time wasting and not being productive; especially for some of us who haven't got spare time to waste (for example, a young mum like myself, of young children with a truck full of to-do lists. Somebody say help me Jesus!). Ok back to business: "Plan", here is another word for vision and God is saying, He will establish all of our visions. Amazing right? How would you feel if God established all your visions? I heard you right; JOYFULL. However, I do want to ask, do you have a vision for your life, family, the coming year? What difference is your life going to make in the world? What kind of life are you working to create and are you intentionally taking steps towards it?

You want God to establish things in your life, first step is to have a vision, make it plain, i.e. have it written down and then commit it to God in faith whilst doing what you can towards that vision. The How? Well that's on God to establish. This is where we get to walk away with much joy because we've place it all in the Father's hands.

Prayer

Father I commit my plans to you today and place them in your hands. I release myself from every burden of thinking that I have to do it all by myself. Thank you that you care for me and that you have set everything up to work for me. As I write my plans down and work towards them, multiply and establish them I pray in Jesus' name, Amen!

Reflections

1. How has this challenged transformed your thinking?
2. What are your plans/visions for your life, family?
3. Are your visions on paper? (if not, they must be written for reference)
4. What steps do you take daily/ regularly towards the vision you have for your life?

STUDY NOTES

DAY 25
The Time Is Now

Introduction

Hey Champions! If your atmosphere is not shifting, your mindset and attitude is not shifting and elevating from before picking up this book, then you might just not be taking the exercises of this challenge seriously. However, today is that day; but you have the choice to make. The time is now! The time is now to give birth to ALL the treasures that are down on the inside of you that the world so desperately needs. Do not short-change or short-circuit yourself. Neither should you look down on yourself for any reason. Where you are right now might not be pleasant. Yes that's facts but we serve a God who does not consult the facts in order to do a new thing. First of all, you are not your situation. Secondly, it is subject to change. You have all it takes! Day 25, Let's get this.

Scripture

John 14:23 (KJV) - "Jesus answered and said unto him, If a man love me, he will keep my words: and my Father will love him, and we will come unto him, and make our abode with him".

Commentary

Does God truly have His abode in you? If God is the source of joy like we learnt already and He has his abode in you, you cannot lack joy or treasures within. Again, joy does not mean that everything is perfect around you. But when God has His abode in you, you see things differently. Your challenges have a different meaning.

What can I do for God to have His abode in me you ask? First of all, you must repent of your sins and ask God into your life. Sin is anything that is not in line with the word of God. Secondly, it is through constant communion with the Father. Communion with God is not just your one time, daily devotion with God or your one time visit to church once a week, no. If you had a friend over for a week, would you schedule a time slot for when you speak to them and that's it? This is how some of us deal with God but that's changing, Amen?

Constant communication, evaluating and placing every thought in front of the mirror of God's word releases peace and joy like nothing else can. However, we must be open, vulnerable and love God enough for this to be fruitful. This is key in order to have our situation and not our situations to have us. I want to encourage you today, to constantly and regularly make time to renew your mind in God's word. This way, your inside will be conducive for the King of all Kings to abide and so the treasures on your inside will bear the kinds of fruit and nutrient the world needs.

Prayer

Father help me to know, realise and feel your presence with me always. I ask for the discipline to align every thought with your word, to evaluate my thoughts and actions through the mirror of your word and to constantly be in communication with you through out each day, in Jesus name, Amen.

Reflections

1. 1.How often do you communicate with God?
2. 2.why is it important to regularly renew our minds in God's Word?

THE 40 DAYS JOY CHALLENGE

STUDY NOTES

DAY 26
Like A Good Tree

Introduction

Welcome to Day 26. Today's challenge is all about evaluating what we're investing our time and energy to and the fruits that those things are bearing. Regular practice of evaluating actions and the fruits they bear is so important to experiencing a joy filled life. If we consider a scenario for example, where someone says something to you very disrespectfully that made you loose your calm in one instance. Having evaluated that incident, you can realise and understand the fruit it bore and determine what you need to do differently in order to keep your joy and peace the next time. It takes practice; however, we cannot master a thing if we don't put the effort in practicing it. Failing at it, is part of the learning. Never beat yourself up for failing. Remember you're still practicing.

Scripture

Matthew 7:17a (NIV) - "Likewise, every good tree bears good fruit"

Commentary

Our text today talks about a good tree and a good fruit. A tree can only bear god fruit when it takes in the right nutrients. So, I ask, what nutrients are you absorbing? What environments are you placing yourself? One thing I've come to realise, is that time wasting really does suck joy out from our lives. If we are honest, we will agree that often, somethings we waste time doing does not actually produce good fruit in us or push us forward into the visions we have for our lives. In order for us to be that 'good tree', we must plant good seeds into our lives and only absorb good nutrients into our hearts. That way, we will be productive and with productivity comes the Joy of accomplishing a worthy task.

Prayer

Heavenly father, we thank you that you have made us to be like a good tree that bears good fruit. Help us therefore Holy Spirit of God to cultivate the discipline and self-control, to only invest time and effort into the things that will only cause our leaves to flourish and our roots to be well rooted in you, Lord, our rock our source and our salvation. This we ask in Jesus name, Amen.

Reflections

1. How often do you take inventory of your actions and what you're putting energy into?
2. Why is it important to practice regular evaluation of our lives and actions?

THE 40 DAYS JOY CHALLENGE

Study Notes

DAY 27
The Value of Good Friendships

Introduction

All I can say is, *What a journey!* God has been faithful, and we are over half way there now. I want to encourage you to keep going. It may be hard but keep going. Your testimony is in your process. Most times we don't like the process. Quite frankly we just want to escape the horrible processes we are often besieged with. However, what I'm learning is that my mindset is what makes all the difference, in a happy situation and in not so great turn of events. I decide if I will let that horrible news or behaviour or past mistakes to affect me. I decide the eyes I look at each circumstance with and the meaning I give it. You can also do the same for your life and the situations you come up against. Most times, it's not about how big or daunting a situation is, but the eyes in which you look at it and the eyes of our understanding is our minds. A great example is David when he fought Goliath. If you can get your mind to believe that it is possible, then it truly becomes possible (See Mark 9:23). 13 days to go. Let's get to our verse for today.

Scripture

Proverbs 27:17 (NIV) - "As iron sharpens iron, so one person sharpens another"

Commentary

You know, we are created to be in regular fellowship with another human being other than ourselves to experience the full expression of abundant and joy-filled life. This is just part of the human make-up. We are not created to live in isolation. One can be easily defeated but not two. Animals for example, often move in herds. There is something to be learnt even in the simple mundane everyday things of life. Infact, it is so dangerous to live in isolation because it creates an environment that lacks the flow of wisdom and re-direction, especially during those times when we are weak. Just like the verse for today, one person sharpens the other. How do you sharpen yourself when YOU are blunt? It doesn't work right?

On the other hand, as important as it is to have friendships to avoid isolation, it is even more important to have good friendships that do sharpen and direct you to the right path for joy to keep flowing in your life. Good friendships sustain joy in your life. There are some people that compound fear, depression, anxiety and worry but there are those that sharpen you and in turn dispel any of these emotions; spurring you on to live out all the greatness that is down on the inside of you. They constantly tell you that all things are working out for you, reminding you that you are loved by the Almighty and that He has not forgotten you; that you will harvest the seeds of your patience, perseverance, love and giving at the appointed time. Therefore, be intentional about your friendships and who you allow to sharpen you.

Prayer

So Father help us to cultivate good and healthy friendships; those ones that will sharpen us in your truth. Help us also to let go of the friendships that simply do not sharpen. That our lives will overflow with joy even in the midst of a challenge because we have been sharpened by another sent by you for us; in Jesus's name, Amen.

Reflections

1. Why is it important to have someone or people that can sharpen you?
2. How do you feel about co- mentorship?
3. After today's challenge, what power do you believe you have, even when faced with a terrible situation?

Study Notes

THE 40 DAYS JOY CHALLENGE

DAY 28

Hold On To What Is Good

Introduction

Welcome to Day 28. I almost can't believe how far we've come and the impact of this challenge on my life. If you've not been following the challenge from the beginning and you just stumbled on this page, I can assure you the devil has tricked you but not anymore. Read up all you have missed, and I know you will be blessed! Why I'm I sure it will bless you? Because none of it is from me. It's all from the Lord God Almighty and all the glory is to Him. So shall we?

Scripture

1 Thessalonians 5:21 (NIV) - "But test them all; hold on to what is good".

Commentary

Today's key text talks about discernment. Yesterday we talked on how important healthy friendships are and how good friendships have the propensity to sustain and promote a joy filled lifestyle. However, even in our friendships and in every other area of our lives, when discernment leads the way, it results to a life in-line with the will of

God and in turn produces joy. God sustains where He leads. So, if you discern His will, stay in it. He provides sustenance for where ever He places you. If you're a Bible scholar, you will know about the story of the Hebrew Boys who were thrown into the fiery furnace with the heat of the fire turned up to its maximum. Long story short, they were sustained because God was leading. Daniel in the Bible is also a great example. When you have discerned from God, stand firm in it even in the midst of opposition. As He sustained Daniel and the Hebrews boys; Shadrach, Meshach and Abednego, He will sustain you also.

Sometimes, we can mis-judge God's Will for us which leads to frustration. God really wants to protect and shield us from frustration and anger and bitterness which is why His Word tells us to get rid of all of these types of emotions from our lives. Why? Because they can actually hinder us from discerning God's will. Our God is a good Father. He knows we cannot function in our highest capacity and unleash our truest potential carrying so much baggage and weights, having to rely on our own understanding. This is why He provides us gifts such as DISCERNMENT, WISDOM and JOY.

If only we can discern where God wants us to be right now, what He wants us to do right now, the work He wants us to put energy into, the decisions He wants us to take, the lifestyle He wants us to live.

Prayer

I pray heavenly Father for grace. Grace to hear you and seek to discern always what you want me to do and say per time in Jesus' name, Amen.

Reflections

1. What do you know about discernment?
2. How important is discernment to you especially after today's challenge?
3. Have you ever prayed for the gift of discernment?
4. What areas of your life can you pray for discernment today?

THE 40 DAYS JOY CHALLENGE

Study Notes

DAY 29
A Praise-full Attitude

Introduction

Welcome to Day 29. Today is all about PRAISE. Our God is fearful in praises (Exodus 15 :11). When was the last time you really praised God as if He had already done the fearful and wonderful thing you really desire? You don't have to believe in God either to have an attitude of thankfulness and gratitude. A brilliant example is Thanksgiving Day in the United States of America (US). Thanksgiving Day is a national holiday celebrated on various dates in the US, Canada and some other participating countries cantered on giving thanks and being grateful. If thanksgiving is that important for a whole nation like the US to literally set aside a day for it, I think as individuals, we can do better to praise God much more regularly. Thanksgiving Day in the US is never cancelled irrespective of the challenges the nation faces. Likewise, we must hold fast a thankful and grateful attitude because, if we truly take time and evaluate, there are more reasons to be grateful than not. I pray today's challenge will get you to praising God and simply being thankful randomly and ALWAYS even without a formal occasion.

Scripture

Psalm 113:3 (NIV) - "From the rising of the sun to the place where it sets, the name of the Lord is to be praised".

Commentary

We just have so much to praise God for. You are reading this book, praise God. You have life, praise Him! You woke up this morning without assistance, praise God! For more motivation to praise, you only need to switch on the news channel, take a visit to an emergency unit at the hospital, visit the prisons, just to name a few. God is faithful. You are blessed and favored amongst many! Please believe that.

So we've talked briefly about Praise and thanksgiving/thankfulness. I really want us to quickly deal with a slight difference between the two. Thankfulness speaks hugely about being thankful for what you have. PRAISE encompasses thankfulness in that it hugely speaks about praising God for what He has done, what He is yet to do and for Who He is.. This is the mountain mover. There's great power in giving God praise for what you cannot see but believe to experience. Much Better, just Praising Him for WHO HE IS; healer, miracle worker, way maker, mountain crusher, head lifter. Can we take a two minutes praise break? Just lift up a praise to God. Tell Him how grateful you are.

I want to share a short testimony with us. At some point this year, I was sick with serious stomach pains; as if my intestines where being twisted. God released a word to PRAISE HIM, and within four minutes of praise, I was completely well; no pains, energy back and most importantly, my joy restored! It was so surreal especially after having gone the whole day (on our wedding anniversary to be precise) in pains. Praise brings victory and with it, JOY. I declare that as you praise Him today, victory will be yours and much joy added to you in Jesus's name, Amen.

Prayer

Father I ask for a garment of praise. Let me be a walking praise cymbal for your glory. I release every weight right now, everything that hinders my praise, I surrender to you now. In Jesus name, Amen.

Reflections

1. When was the last time you praised God like He has already made your desires come true?
2. Write down every situation that could hinder your praise and one by one release and commit them to God verbally while you praise God.

THE 40 DAYS JOY CHALLENGE

Study Notes

THE 40 DAYS JOY CHALLENGE

DAY 30
Faith; your anchor

Introduction

rumroll pleasee It's Day 30! How did we get here? Only by God's grace and through determination. My utmost desire would be that as a result of you picking up this book and following the challenge up until now, that your mindset is being re-programmed for your favour and for you to stand out. Today we're looking at faith as an anchor. If you're thinking, 'well what is that?' Well stick around to the end of today's challenge and hopefully that question will be answered.

Scripture

Hebrews 6 :19: 'We have this hope as an anchor for the soul, firm and secure. It enters the inner sanctuary behind the curtain.

Commentary

Faith is one of the secret ingredients to the growth in my walk with God. So, what is Faith? According to the dictionary, faith is the *complete trust or confidence in something or someone*. I dare say that this definition was derived from the Bible definition of faith which simply put, is choosing to believe that Jesus Christ is who He said He is, even though we haven't yet seen Him with our physical eyes.

108

Why is faith important? It's important because it is our push-back fire. When those circumstances, health incidents, delays and thoughts come to hunt and attack, our faith is our shield that pushes all the effects right back from hurting, destroying, pulling us down and stealing our JOY! (*See Ephesians 6:16*). Where should we place our faith? Our faith should be built and secured in the name of Jesus and in His word. These are the only components that will never change. Every other thing in life is subject to change and but a sinking sand. Investors would advice that should you want to choose a worthwhile investment, factors such as value and yield play a huge part. If we apply the same principle in placing our faith in God's word, the value includes a trust worthy word that is imperishable which revives our soul, (see psalm 19:7). The yield is immeasurable, even to eternal life (see Mark 10: 29-30).

To keep it short, sadly we have ALL gone through trying and difficult situations. But the hard truth is that, it is not what happened to you but how you look at and deal with what happened to you. Secondly, what happened to you does not determine your destiny- it doesn't have the final say. All the circumstances may be against you. Don't worry. God is for you. In His word, He promises this. What we must understand also is that God does not need to consult our situation or circumstance in order to turn things around. He is not limited by our natural circumstances. He is Super natural.

You know what has helped me keep my head above the water? My strong FAITH in God. I believe His Word, especially those He has revealed or spoken to me specifically and I hold Him to it regardless of what is going on around me. I want to encourage you in today, to build your FAITH up. It's part of our armour and what does it look like for a soldier who is in a battle-field to be without his full armour?

Prayer

Heavenly father I ask for the gift of faith to rise up greatly within me; that I will always speak blessings even when I don't see it, that I will speak victory instead of defeat. I pray for discipline to listen and read your word (Bible) often as your word in *Romans 10:17* tells me that faith comes by hearing your word. I ask for grace father to grow my faith in you, in Jesus name, Amen.

Reflections

1. What does faith in God mean to you?
2. What can you do today to start building your faith?

Study Notes

DAY 31
All of God's goodness is yours

Introduction

Welcome to Day 31. I'm genuinely excited for you; for the change that you are about to experience or experiencing already, the ease you will find in situations that once caused you to loose your peace. This is my mission; that as many people that I'm able to reach, that they live their lives with the right perspective, in wholeness and in freedom. With just 9 days to go, I can only pray that this mission is accomplished.

Scripture

Exodus 33:19 (NKJV) - "And he said, "I will make all my goodness pass before you and will proclaim before you my name 'The LORD'. And I will be gracious to whom I will be gracious, and will show mercy on whom I will show mercy"

Commentary

Who can deny that God's goodness has not passed before them in all of their lifetime? The truth is that, God's goodness is everywhere, even in the situations that seem grim and dead. Where we miss it is not seeing the good in the midst of the pain, the miracle in the midst of the mess. Whatever we focus on multiplies. Our brains somehow stick more with negative and bad thoughts and then all that we are filled with is that God has forgotten us, the situation will never change, God doesn't love us, God doesn't hear us, God doesn't care or even God is not who He says He is. I've come to dispel that lie and to encourage you to look again. God's hand has always been on YOU and preserved you through it all. When God said '*let there be light*', the earth was dark and without form and void. However, God didn't look at the circumstance around to determine if light was possible. He spoke the word and light came rushing forth! In the same way, God has called you blessed, regardless of who likes you or not, the family you come from, the economy, your past mistakes. Every voice tells you that you're stuck, you can never rise from this, you can never achieve that goal in the natural. Well, the good news once again is that we serve a Super-natural God.

I want to share a scenario with us that happens during planting. When a farmer plants, more likely than not, weeds are going to appear alongside the fruit of the produce they have planted. Does the farmer sit there and think, ohh, look at all these weeds, there is no good anymore of the fruit that has been produced? NO! He grabs his increase and keeps it stepping in joy. We also need to have the same attitude. This is how your river of joy keeps flowing.

Prayer

Heavenly Father, I surrender my seemingly impossible situations to you, the God of impossibilities. I pray that the eyes of my understanding be opened and enlightened to see all of your mercies daily, to recount your faithfulness Lord and to focus on them, in Jesus' name, Amen.

Reflections

1. Think of a difficult situation you are facing right now and find the goodness and favour of God in that same situation.
2. List at least 3 good things that happened in your life yesterday and give God thanks for them

Study Notes

DAY 32
Like Stars forever and ever

Introduction

Welcome to Day 32. 8 days to go! I'm amazed at how far we've come on this journey. It's truly been through God's grace and I'm super thankful to Him. It's been a huge learning process as well. Who believes with me that our God is greater; greater than any goliath we are facing now or that we will face in the future? The aim of this challenge is to encourage you to hold on to your joy, that at the end of it all, you will see that all things have been working together for your good. The strategy of the devil is one, to cause you to doubt the potency of God and two, to cause you to loose your peace. Don't give in to the enemy. The God who spoke worlds into being is for you. He's on your side. Do not be discouraged by the setbacks and ugly situations. God will make things happen that will amaze you; just like stars forever and ever, you will shine.

Scripture

Daniel 12:3 (NIV) - "Those who are wise will shine like the brightness of the heavens, and those who lead many to righteousness, like the stars for ever and ever"-

Commentary

Our verse for today talks about those who are *wise*. A person who is wise is a person who acts in wisdom. What is wisdom? Wisdom isn't simply intelligence or knowledge or understanding. It is knowing what to do per time and actually doing it. It's not enough to know and not act upon it because if nothing is done, nothing is changed and nothing is produced.

Many times, we actually know the right thing to do but somehow, we don't do it because of fear; fear we will be misunderstood, fear of failure, fear of people, fear of being judged, or simply fear of the unknown. Our own thoughts may even talk us out from doing the right thing and taking the right step. However, the Bible tells us that it is the fear and knowledge of God that brings wisdom and insight; not the fear of these other things.

If you know God, His wisdom is available to you. God is the source of Wisdom. Nothing is a surprise to Him and He knows what you should be doing at each point, where you need to be, what you need to say and not say. All you have to do is ask Him and be open to receive. The Bible in James 1:5(NIV) says, *'If any of you lacks wisdom, you should ask God, who gives generously to all without finding fault, and it will be given to you'*. God is always ready to provide His wisdom to you for you to be a LIGHT, for you to SHINE and ultimately to live the life He truly intended for you; a joy-filled life!

Prayer

Father help me to seek your wisdom always, that I will not act from my own will or intelligence but will seek your leading. Help me also to obey and to act upon the instructions you give me so that joy will remain in my heart and life, in Jesus' name, AMEN.

Reflections

1. Why do you think some of us know what to do but we don't take the necessary action?
2. List down 5 or more areas of your life where there is fear
3. Pray and ask God to provide wisdom in those specific areas

THE 40 DAYS JOY CHALLENGE

Study Notes

THE 40 DAYS JOY CHALLENGE

DAY 33
Revelation over Information

Introduction

Welcome to Day 33. Wow God is being glorified! If you just picked up this book and landed on today, I just want to ask you a few questions. Are there things in your life contesting your joy, your sanity, your peace, your sound mind, your testimony about God and your pursuit to know God more? Well this entire book is for you and especially, today's challenge. The majority of us haven't realised how POWERFUL joy is. Without joy, you are limited. The Bible tells us that we draw strength from joy. Without joy, there is no strength to push forward and this is what the enemy desires; that you stop, that you don't see good, that you stay down and depressed, that you stay in darkness and anxiety and worry, living a life of regret. However, with this challenge, we serve a notice to the agenda of the devil in our world and in our lives and we decree, it is finished! We will fulfil purpose and we will win. We will not stop but continue to press forward. We will not be silent but continue to speak God's blessings and promises over our lives. God is full of mercy and full of surprises. The Lord God Almighty is still at work in your life. Our Lives will be joy-filled because we live and move in the knowledge of who we are in the eyes of the Father, His plan for us; GOOD, and the revelation of who our God is.

Scripture

Ephesians 1:17 (NIV) - "I keep asking that the God of our Lord Jesus Christ, the glorious Father, may give you the Spirit of wisdom and revelation, so that you may know Him better".

Commentary

We talked about wisdom yesterday. Today we are looking at revelation as a seed for a joyful life. Our God is infinite, self-existing. He is immutable, never changing. He is self-sufficient, omnipotent, omnipresent and omniscient. With just these points, I wish to tender to you that with the revelation of who this Mighty Being really is, at least as much as the humanin brain allows us to imagine, it is impossible not to have joy in our hearts. What revelation of God are you holding on to? Do you have any revelation of who God is?

Joy is a decision. It's a decision to go after God, to stand firm in His word, to seek His presence and a revelation of who He is in order to draw from his attributes. Joy is a fruit of the spirit of God. Can a tree bear fruit that it doesn't have the seed for? God is our tree of joy and only in Him can we draw this joy to keep us going in a very difficult world and in trying times.

Prayer

Heavenly Father, the God of our Lord Jesus Christ. The glorious one, I pray for the Spirit of wisdom and revelation, that I may know you and the power of your resurrection. That I may walk in your GLORY, in your JOY and in your LOVE, in Jesus' name, Amen.

Reflection

1. What is your revelation of who God is?
2. What is your revelation of who you are in the eyes of God?

Study Notes

THE 40 DAYS JOY CHALLENGE

DAY 34
Overflow With Hope

Introduction

Welcome to Day 34. When I say I'm in awe? This challenge could not have gotten this far without God, without joy in my heart, without discipline, without everything we've pretty much looked at in this challenge and I'm so thankful. This is for YOU! And I pray that it has impacted you and truly given you a different perspective on the journey of life and the best way to tackle the challenges that will come.

Scripture

Romans 15:13 (NIV) - "May the God of hope fill you with all joy and peace as you trust in him, so that you may overflow with hope by the power of the Holy Spirit."

Commentary

HOPE is a powerful source of joy. We've used and commonised the word *hope* so much so that we've forgotten the power of hope. I'm sure you've heard people casually say, 'oh I *hope* it doesn't rain today' without necessarily attaching any real meaning to that hope. We hear people say, 'I *hope* this happens or that happens'. Well let's

THE 40 DAYS JOY CHALLENGE

look at what the Bible says about hope. 1 Corinthians 13:13a says. *'And now these three remain: faith, hope and love'.* Hope is eternal. God created hope on the inside of each and every human being. God wants us to stir up that hope on the inside of us through the channel of faith and joy. Put hope in front of God's promise over your life. Hope is the oil that keeps the engine of joy running and flowing. Hope is that force that makes you adamant in not allowing your situation, environment or condition to determine or dictate your JOY or your future. Why? Because it's not in the hands of those things. Hope creates vision.

Do not give up my friend. Do not loose hope. People may tell you that you will get disappointed if you keep on hoping but the Bible tells us that a heart without hope is *'sick'* (Proverbs 13:12a). Yes it hurts, it's painful, it's difficult, it's dark, it's unfair but we must understand that God sees differently than we do and when it's time to turn your situation around, He wouldn't need to consult the experts, the doctors, the economy, your family background, upbringing, race or gender to bless you. He is God all by Himself and besides Him, there is none other. You are His workmanship created for good works! That means, through the help of the Holy Spirit, you can turn a mess into a miracle. The magic power (greatness) is in you. Let our verse today be the prayer, that God Himself, will fill us with an overflow of hope. Believe that when you ask genuinely, that you have received and watch your mindset change and strength return. Arhh! I hope you get this through the help of the Holy spirit.

Prayer

So Heavenly Father, just like the verse for today, I ask that you Almighty God, fill me with all joy and peace that my hope will overflow even in the face of opposition, adversity and contradictory facts. Lord I know you are faithful. You bring the promises to pass in your timing and in your way and when you do, it is exceedingly, abundantly, above all we can think or imagine. In this I place my hope today and always, in Jesus name, Amen.

Reflections

1. What does it mean to Hope on God?
2. What are you hoping on God for today?
3. What are the challenges of hoping on God?
4. Do you have something that you see every day to keep God's promise alive in your life and your hopes strong?

Study Notes

THE 40 DAYS JOY CHALLENGE

DAY 35
Stretch Your Boundaries

Introduction

Welcome to Day 35. I'm still in awe! Don't forget this is not just theoretical information. This is a revelation that changed my life and I had to share it with you. Friends, this thing is REAL. JOY breaks the power of a 'bad' situation to pull you down and cause you to stop. You have the power to let your JOY make that situation so insignificant that there is no other option for it to change in your favour. We will finish well, our lives will shine, we will fulfil purpose, we will not loose hope, our JOY will remain. Day 35 let's get to it.

Scripture

John 10 :10 - " The thief comes only to steal and kill and destroy; I have come that they may have life and have it in full".

Commentary

Life in full is a joy filled life! That is God's intention. Whatever the agenda of the enemy over your life, God's agenda overrides it. One way we live life in full is by stretching our boundaries. There are abilities we are yet to tap into. Do you truly believe that? I don't know about you but I want a life of no regrets when I meet the

128

90year old me. Have you thought about that? Would there be things the 90year old you would wish you did?

To stretch your boundaries, you must be willing to try new things, invest in yourself, grow, keep moving and simply embrace change.

Prayer

Father help me to truly live my life in full; to tap into all that you have placed in me and not grow weary in moving and reaching for more, in Jesus' name, AMEN .

Reflections

1. Would the 90-year-old you commend the decisions you're making today?
2. What can you do today that stretches your boundaries?

THE 40 DAYS JOY CHALLENGE

Study Notes

THE 40 DAYS JOY CHALLENGE

DAY 36
It's subject to change

Introduction

Welcome to Day 36. All I can say is, " *this God is too good oo*". Who knows this song? I actually did a cover for this song recently on my YouTube Channel at AmakaToby TV - feel free to go check it out if you haven't already.

I want to encourage you today, never loose heart my friend. Whatever situation you're currently facing is subject to change. Isn't that a wonderful testimony? Often times, it's difficult for us to embrace change because it disturbs our comfort zone. However, growth is a function of change. Knowledge is a function of change. Change is also good and the change coming your way will be a pleasant one! God is for you. He knows what He's doing and has promised to sail the ship of our lives to an expected end. So, sit back and be JOYFUL! Alright, let's get to our verse for the day.

Scripture

Mathew 8:26 (NIV) - "He replied, 'You of little faith, why are you so afraid?' Then He got up and rebuked the winds and the waves, and it was completely calm".

Commentary

While in my quiet time, the Holy Spirit said to me that what Jesus got up to do, i.e rebuking the winds and bringing calmness back, the disciples had the power and authority to do also if only they had faith and exercised it. How often, we modern day disciples do the same? Don't we hand over fear to things around us instead of standing u and serving that thing faith! Faith dispels fear. Fear causes us to put limits on even the visions and potentials down on the inside of us by making us focus on our present condition. However today, I want to challenge you to exchange every fear with faith. When fear rings the bell again, let faith open the door, so that you can experience all the beauty you were created to experience; living a fulfilled life and having joy as the icing on the cake, Amen!

Prayer

Heavenly Father, thank you for leaving your spirit with us. Thank you for your love. Thank you for giving me all that I need to live a life of courage, boldness and joy. I ask for grace to break out from every limiting thought that tries to keep me from my destiny; that I will let my faith rise and answer the door when fear and doubt knocks, in Jesus name, Amen

Reflections

1. Why is it often easy for us to sit with and accept limiting thoughts?
2. What fears do you have right now that you can exchange with faith?
3. Why is it sometimes easier for us to accept fear than faith?

Study Notes

THE 40 DAYS JOY CHALLENGE

THE 40 DAYS JOY CHALLENGE

DAY 37
Look up

Introduction

Hi There! Welcome to Day 37. Seriously, if you have made it this far, you are already a Champion because I'm pretty sure you have had to fight to keep your joy till this moment.

Can we have testimony time please? This challenge has not been easier than it is now and I can't believe we are coming close to the end. I can only attribute it to GRACE. Lets' talk about God's Grace. Grace is DIVINE ABILITY. There are some things that in our might and ability, are impossible to rise from or to solve. However, when God's Grace steps in, you wonder, how did I get out or recover from this mess? God gives an amount of grace to each and every one of us to turn the table right on top of that thing that came to take you out! This is what I'm serving my world today and inviting YOU to tap into daily! . . . I still can't believe it's Day 37. Let's get to it.

Scripture

Isaiah 60:5a (NIV) - "Then you will look and be radiant, your heart will throb and swell with joy".

136

Commentary

Our verse for today is simply straight! If only we can see right, our hearts will literally explode with joy. Many times, we don't see right. Many times, we only look downwards when we should be looking up. In the popular story of Jesus raising Lazarus from death, Jesus didn't look down at Lazarus' dead body, the stones, the stench from Lazarus being dead for days. According to John 11 verse 41, the Bible records that *Jesus looked up*. I want to challenge you today to look up. Quit focusing on your environment. Make room for God to do a new thing!

One way to know you're not seeing right is looking and feeling fear, depressed or simply not seeing any good that can come out from what you're facing. I want to challenge you today to lift up your eyes and SEE. You are not your condition, situation or circumstance. You are separate from what happened to you or what is happening to you and the power is all yours to see right, work that thing until it becomes a testimony as your heart explodes in joy and thanksgiving!

Prayer

Father I ask for grace to see where I am right, that it is simply a set up for your glory, in Jesus' name, Amen.

Reflections

1. Have you discovered the grace upon your life?
2. What in your life right now can you look at differently and find God's hand in?

Study Notes

THE 40 DAYS JOY CHALLENGE

DAY 38
The God of The Impossible

Introduction

Welcome to Day 38. Two days to go! I want to say a big THANK YOU. Thank you for sticking through this journey with me. I really do hope it's been insightful, inspirational and transformational. I hope you're seeing changes already in your mindset, in the way you view situations and the kinds of thought you allow to take root. I'm eager to hear your testimonials. Please write to me; details on how to write to me can be found towards the end of this book. Leave your review if this challenge has changed your life and mindset for the better. It would be my pleasure to hear from you. In the meantime, let's get on with Day 38.

Scripture

Zephaniah 3:17 (NIV) - "The LORD your God is with you, the Mighty Warrior who saves. He will take great delight in you, in his love he will no longer rebuke you, but will rejoice over you with singing."

Commentary

What a Word hey? It's God's desire to look over our lives and REJOICE!. You know the moment you received Christ as your Lord and Saviour, the Mighty One came into your life to do all the things our verse for today says. You have come into a new kingdom. You have the Creator of heaven and earth in and around you. He's for you, fighting for you to *'exult over you with loud singing'*. Oh Hallelujah!.

Our God is the God of the impossible. He turns impossible situations into stories of His faithfulness. Remember from the Bible the story of David, Joseph, Daniel, Esther. Impossible and dark situations are but setups; for God to do the miraculous, if we will release the burden of them to Him. I pray you will do that today and walk away with joy indescribable, because that is your portion and inheritance.

Prayer

Father thank you for your Word that brings Joy, your Word that leads me. I want to meditate on it every day and every moment so that I don't miss the treasures and the JOY that you have generously given. I pray that it transforms me so that every day, I become more like you in Jesus' name, Amen!

Reflections

1. 1.What impossible situation do you have in your life right now that you can lift to God?

2. 2.Have you prayed about them? (If not, don't get weary in praying until that situation turns to your favour)

THE 40 DAYS JOY CHALLENGE

Study Notes

THE 40 DAYS JOY CHALLENGE

DAY 39
Make a Decision And Stick To It

Introduction

Welcome to Day 39! I can't believe we only have one more day to go in this journey. How did this all happen? All I can say is that it's through a decision and by the GRACE of God. You never know what you can do until you make a decision, stick to it and allow God. No matter what the odds look like, be confident that God and you are a MAJORITY and run with that thing! Who's ready for Day 39?

Scripture

James 3:16 (NIV) - "For wherever there is jealousy and selfish ambition, there you will find disorder and evil of every kind.

Commentary

Jealousy and selfishness are seeds for everything evil. We must know that jealousy or selfishness doesn't stop God from lifting the other person because God has a million ways to bring about a thing. However, jealousy and selfishness robs the person harbouring them. We may not realise it but it's not hurting anyone else but the person harbouring them. Most especially, we cannot experience true and lasting joy carrying the heavy load of jealousy

144

and selfishness on the inside of us. Be trustworthy, be a person of integrity, be loving, be a person that can be counted on. I pray that as this challenge is drawing to a close, that you will purge yourself of any jealousy or selfishness, so that the floodgates of heaven will be open towards you and that you will experience a life filled with joy and peace.

Prayer

Dear Heavenly Father, you created me out of JOY. When you made me, you said that I am perfect. If there is anything that is not from you that has grown in me, I ask that you cut it off. I want my life to be a reflection of your image, in Jesus' name, Amen!

Reflections

1. 1.How can one overcome jealousy and selfishness?
2. 2.What character traits can you replace for jealousy and selfishness?
3. 3.What can you do to ensure that your inside is free from jealousy and selfishness?

THE 40 DAYS JOY CHALLENGE

Study Notes

DAY 40
Put in the work

Introduction

Welcome to Day 40! This is it Guys! If you could see my heart, I'm actually moon walking right now in thanks to God. I say in my heart because I might not be able to pull it off for real but anyway, God looks at the heart. I'm so thankful, I can't even express how much! God is FAITHFUL and He is a Good Good Father. He loves us and cares for us. He is the only one that never fails. All we need to do is play our part. Yes, we do have a part to play. John 13 : 8b says, '*Jesus answered, unless I wash you, you have no part with me*'. How Well are you playing your part? Are you just blaming God or your situation for everything? We must do what is in our power for God to do what is beyond our power. Ok, for the last time. Let's get this Day 40.

Scripture

Proverbs 22:29 - "Do you see someone skilled in their work? They will serve before kings; they will not serve before officials of low rank" .

Commentary

How well are you working to be skilled at what you do? You know,

THE 40 DAYS JOY CHALLENGE

Laziness and procrastination are enemies to being skilled. For example, the greatest footballers of our time; Ronaldo, Messi. Yes, they maybe gifted but to be skilled, they will agree that it needs work, practice, determination and constant improvement. How are you working to improve your craft? To improve what you do, to serve better? Because at the heart of joy is service. Why? Because the joy you have is the joy you will serve anyone that comes around you. Therefore, I want to encourage you to put in work on your craft and not procrastinate in order to serve before kings which is a metaphor really for joy.

We don't work to be skilled just for people to see how good we are and to congratulate us. That's ok but God is after something much more. It's about letting God's glory to be seen through us. It's about us becoming an example of God's goodness. I want to encourage you to keep honoring God, keep working in humility to be skilled, God himself will endorse you and make you stand out. He will show people Himself, who you really are.

Prayer

Heavenly Father, I thank you that you are faithful. You never fail even when I fail. I want to honour you. I want to have a part with you. Wash off everything in me that hinders me from having a part with you. I repent of my sins. Lord you are my strength. I cast off the spirit of procrastination and put on the grace for accomplishment. I will no longer have unfinished work or unrealised ideas. I will be fervent and diligent. I will serve and work

THE 40 DAYS JOY CHALLENGE

to be skilled at my craft; being a blessing to those around me and my world, in Jesus name, Amen.

Reflections

1. How do you view JOY in the world we live in?
2. What have you learnt about JOY from this challenge?
3. What measures are you putting in place to keep joy flowing in your life?
4. How Well are you playing your part to live in Joy?

Study Notes

THE 40 DAYS JOY CHALLENGE

THE 40 DAYS JOY CHALLENGE

PERSONAL THANK YOU NOTE

Thank you from the bottom of my heart, for investing and picking up my book, for taking the time to read and for taking the steps needed to live a life of JOY, PEACE, FREDDOM and ABUNDNACE. Thank you for sticking through this journey with me. It's been insightful, encouraging, growing and JOYFUL; at least for me. I pray it's been the same and much more for YOU!

If this challenge has inspired you in anyway, could you please let me know? I'm eager to know that I haven't gone through this intense journey with no impact. You can write me via my Facebook Page at AMAKATOBY TV or via my Instagram page, @mrs_amaka_o. I can't wait to hear about all that this book births through you and celebrate with you; giving glory to God!

I hope that my mission to encourage a joy-filled lifestyle through this 40 Days Joy Challenge is fruitful. I pray that you live in such a way that you capture joy, you consciously seek it daily employing the different elements we've discussed in this book and fighting for it when it seems joy is being drowned by your circumstances.

AMAKATOBY TV RESOURCES

Be on the lookout for many more materials coming soon from myself and from AmakaToby TV Ministries. Subscribe to AmakaToby TV on YouTube for regular inspirational and motivational videos. The ministry commissioned to myself and husband is one of expansion of the Kingdom of God and a full realisation of the potentials of God's beloved children. If you wish to partner or work with AmakaToby TV Ministries, you can do so by contacting us at info@amakatobytv.com. You can also reach us on AmakaToby TV on Facebook, Amakatobytv.com, @mrs_amaka_o on Instagram, AmakaToby TV on twitter and Amaka Toby Tv on YouTube.

About Author

AMAKA OGBONNA- author, speaker, and counsellor- has a passion for people; especially young people and women and for helping them form the right mindsets and perspectives in order to truly live freely and joyfully. She also has a very strong presence across all her social media platforms of nearly 1,000 followers currently. In her media platforms, she shares her passion for God and making a positive difference in people's lives; encouraging them to pursue and realise their fullest potentials. She is the director and founder of a YouTube Series titled: *Woman You Are Necessary*. Amaka, together with her husband Toby are in leadership position in their local church. Amaka is also the proud mother of two precious jewels; Diamond and Samuel. For more information, visit www.amakatobytv.com

THE 40 DAYS JOY CHALLENGE

THE 40 DAYS JOY CHALLENGE

THE 40 DAYS JOY CHALLENGE

THE 40 DAYS JOY CHALLENGE

Printed in Poland
by Amazon Fulfillment
Poland Sp. z o.o., Wrocław

60310160R00106